Explore!
STONE, BRONZE
and IRON AGES

Sonya Newland

WAYLAND
www.waylandbooks.co.uk

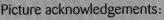

First published in Great Britain in 2015 by Wayland

Copyright © Wayland, 2015

Dewey number 936.1'01-dc23
ISBN: 9780750295499
10 9 8 7 6 5 4 3 2 1

Wayland
An imprint of Hachette Children's Group
Part of Hodder & Stoughton
Carmelite House
50 Victoria Embankment
London EC4Y 0DZ

An Hachette UK Company
www.hachette.co.uk

www.hachettechildrens.co.uk

A catalogue record for this title is available from the
British Library

Printed in China

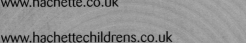

Produced for Wayland by
White-Thomson Publishing Ltd
www.wtpub.co.uk

Editor: Sonya Newland
Designer: Ian Winton
Picture researcher: Sonya Newland
Illustrations: Stefan Chabluk
Wayland editor: Annabel Stones

Picture acknowledgements:
The author and publisher would like to thank the
following agencies and people for allowing these
pictures to be reproduced:

Cover background Tooykrub/Shutterstock; cover icon
and title background Kudryashka/Shutterstock; cover top
Andreas Praefcke/Wikimedia; cover middle Michel Wal/
Wikimedia; cover bottom Justin Black/Shutterstock;
p.1 (left) Jonathan Cardy/Wikimedia; (right) jaroslava V/
Shutterstock; p.3 Andreas Praefcke/Wikimedia; p.4 jps/
Shutterstock; p.5 (top) Wolfgang Sauber/Wikimedia;
(bottom) Johnbod/Wikimedia; p.7 (top) Matthew Ashton/
AMA/Corbis; (bottom) nicolasprimola/iStock; p.8
Rameessos/Wikimedia; p.9 (top) Didier Descouens/
Wikimedia; (bottom) Martin Zwick/age footstock/
Superstock; p.10 Creative Nature Media/Shutterstock;
p.11 (top) lowefoto/Alamy; (bottom) Terry Yarrow/
Shutterstock; p.12 Jule_Berlin/Shutterstock; p. 13 (top)
Herby/Wikimedia; (bottom) David Peter Robinson/
Shutterstock; p.14 North Wind Picture Archives/
Alamy; p.15 (top) Dorling Kindersley/Getty Images;
(bottom) Radka1/Shutterstock; p.16 John Kepchar/
Shutterstock; p.17 (top) Rama/Wikimedia; (bottom)
Sailko/Wikimedia; p.18 Dr Peter Hoare/Wikimedia; p.19
(top) Von Falkenstein/Wikimedia; (bottom) Luis García;
p.20 Jonathan Cardy/Wikimedia; p.21 (top) fotoVoyager/
iStock; (bottom) Stefano Bianchetti/Corbis; p.22 jaroslava
V/Shutterstock; p.23 (top) dtopal/Shutterstock; (bottom)
Janine Lamontagne /iStock; p.24 DaveKav/Wikimedia;
p.25 (top) © Hartmann Linge, Wikimedia Commons,
CC-by-sa 3.0; (bottom) Andreas Praefcke; p.26 (top) ©
Hartmann Linge, Wikimedia Commons, CC-by-sa 3.0;
p.28 (top) Terry Yarrow/Shutterstock; (middle) dtopal/
Shutterstock; (bottom) nicolasprimola/iStock; p.29
jaroslava V/Shutterstock; p.31 (top) Johnbod/Wikimedia;
(bottom) Sailko/Wikimedia.

Contents

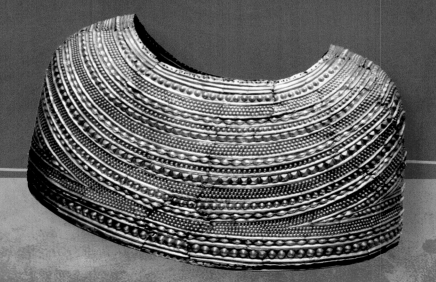

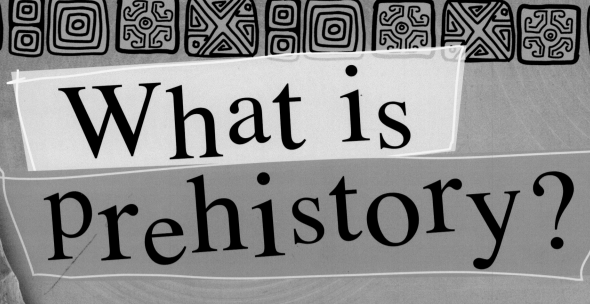

What is prehistory?

Humans have lived on Earth for more than two million years, but for many thousands of years they had no written language. This long period is called 'prehistory'. Historians divide prehistory into three eras, named after the main material people used to make things.

The Stone Age

The Stone Age began about 2.5 million years ago. This was when the first people on Earth began making tools and weapons out of stone to help them survive. Later in the Stone Age, early humans began to use other materials for making these items, such as wood and the skin and bones of animals.

Early people used different types of stone and rock for their weapons. This is a dagger made from a hard rock called flint.

The Bronze Age

The Bronze Age began around 2500BCE, when people first began using the metals copper, tin and bronze. More people arrived in Britain from Europe, and they began to live in permanent settlements instead of moving around all the time. Bronze Age people developed new ways of farming and metalworking.

The discovery of metal meant that people could make stronger tools and weapons, like these bronze axe heads.

The Celts made beautiful jewellery, including brooches, bracelets and heavy neck rings like this, called torcs.

The Iron Age

A new age began about 800BCE, when people started using iron. Iron Age people – known as Celts – lived in tribes led by a king or queen. After the Romans invaded Britain in 43CE, Celtic traditions and beliefs began to mix with Roman ones. The Romans could read and write, so their arrival in Britain marks the end of the Iron Age and the point where prehistory becomes history.

The prehistoric world

Prehistoric Earth did not look much like it does today. A million years ago, Britain was joined to Europe by an area of land called Doggerland. In the middle of the Stone Age, Doggerland flooded over and Britain became an island.

North Sea

Doggerland

Rhine

Thames

Channel

This map shows what Britain may have looked like in the early Stone Age.

Ice Ages

Throughout Earth's history, there have been long periods called Ice Ages, when the climate was freezing cold and the land was covered in glaciers. It would have been tough for humans to survive in these conditions. However, we know that people moved around Britain in the warmer periods between the Ice Ages because archaeologists have found evidence such as simple stone tools and human bones.

The Stone Age landscape

As the climate changed, so did the face of the Earth. In between the Ice Ages, most of Britain was covered in grassland. After the last Ice Age, about 11,500 years ago, thick forests spread across Britain and the land was dotted with lakes – the remains of the glaciers. Later, humans cleared the trees to make way for their villages and farms.

The remains of a prehistoric forest were uncovered on a beach in Wales during a storm in 2014. These tree stumps are more than 5,000 years old.

Animals

Changes in the climate affected the plants and animals that could be found in Britain. In the early Stone Age, large beasts such as lions, rhinos, elephants and mammoths roamed the country. Later, many of these big creatures died out and smaller animals such as reindeer and wild cattle were more common.

Woolly rhinoceroses lived in southern England and Doggerland even during the freezing Ice Ages.

Food and Farming

For thousands of years, people's lives were ruled by the basic need to find food. Early Stone Age people spent their days hunting animals and gathering plants and berries in order to survive. When new settlers from Europe brought farming methods to Britain, it changed the way humans lived dramatically.

Hunter-gatherers

In the early Stone Age (known as the Paleolithic era), humans moved around almost constantly, following the herds of animals such as deer that they hunted for meat. Larger animals like mammoths, which were harder to kill with stone spears, would be chased over cliffs or into bogs. Prehistoric hunter-gatherers did not only eat meat – their diet also included fish, insects, vegetables, fruit and nuts.

Ancient cave paintings show how important animals and hunting were to early humans.

Managed hunting

Around the middle of the Stone Age (the Mesolithic era), people began to move around less than they had before. They were still hunter-gatherers, but they hunted in a different way – clearing areas of woodland near a water source and catching the animals that came to drink there. If they were careful not to kill too many beasts from a herd, they could stay in one place for a few months.

Prehistoric rivers teemed with fish, which people caught using harpoons made of bone like these.

The first farmers

By around 4000BCE – the start of the Neolithic era, or New Stone Age – humans had worked out how to grow their own food by planting crops. They began to tame wild animals such as boar, so they could be bred for meat. Farming was hard work because tools were still very simple objects made of stone and bone, but for the first time people had a steady source of food and could settle permanently in one place.

At the Knap of Howar in Scotland, Stone Age farmers grew barley and wheat, and bred sheep and pigs.

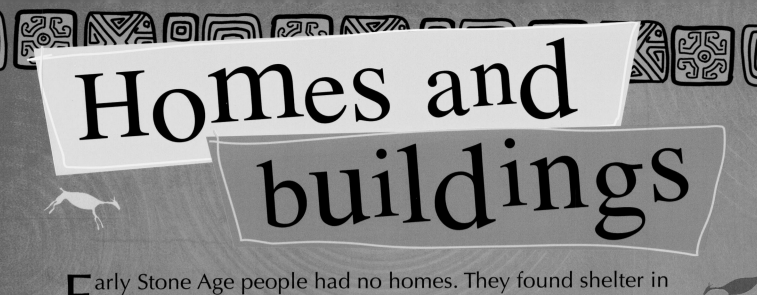

Homes and buildings

Early Stone Age people had no homes. They found shelter in caves when they needed to, but most of the time they lived in the open air, going wherever the herds went. As time passed and lifestyles changed, prehistoric people learnt how to construct different buildings to meet their needs.

Stone Age huts

Archaeologists have discovered an amazing Mesolithic site near a peat bog at Star Carr in Yorkshire. Many artefacts have been found there, including the remains of a hut built by Stone Age settlers. It had a frame made of wooden posts, and walls of mud mixed with straw. The people who lived there covered the floor inside with moss or reeds from the lake.

Stone Age settlers may have covered their huts with animal skins.

A Bronze Age monument

One of the most famous Bronze Age sites is Flag Fen in Peterborough. Here, prehistoric people built a huge causeway and platform. The causeway was made up of over 60,000 wooden posts driven into the ground and covered with thousands of wooden planks. No one knows for sure what Flag Fen was built for, but it might have been a place for ancient people to worship their gods.

The wood that was used to build Flag Fen was oak. Oak trees did not grow in this area, so it must have been transported from a long way away.

Iron Age hill forts

By the Iron Age, people had split into tribes that were often at war with one another. To protect themselves from attack, some tribes built fortified settlements the top of hills. From high hill forts like Hambledon Hill in Dorset, they could see their enemy approaching from a long way off. Ditches and banks of earth were dug into the sides of the hill to make it hard to climb.

Hambledon Hill hill fort was built around 2,500 years ago and was nearly 200 metres high.

Family and society

Historians think that even the earliest Stone Age people lived in family groups. There was safety in numbers and it was easier for people to hunt down large animals if they worked in groups. Even so, these bands of hunter-gatherers were small – in the middle of the Stone Age, only about 3,000 people lived in Britain.

A Neolithic community

Archaeologists have learnt a lot about Stone Age societies by studying a group of eight Neolithic houses at Skara Brae in Orkney. These houses are all about the same size and they share a basic sewer system. This suggests that there was no leader – everyone was considered equal. It also shows that the people who lived there worked together as a community.

The houses at Skara Brae all have just one room, with a stone fireplace for heating and cooking.

Bronze Age society

By the Bronze Age, people were moving around less than they had in the Stone Age. They stayed in one place for longer, growing crops and raising animals for meat. Settlements were larger, although communities were usually still built on family ties. There began to be a social divide between the skilled metalworkers and those who could not make things to trade with their neighbours.

On Dartmoor, there are the remains of 24 circular Bronze Age huts, inside a huge outer wall.

Iron Age tribes

By the time the Romans invaded, there were around 30 tribes in Britain. Each tribe was led by a king, or sometimes a queen. Beneath them were the nobles – the landowners and the greatest warriors. Next in importance were the priests (called druids) and the craftsmen. Finally there were the ordinary people – the tribesmen who farmed and hunted for food.

Celts lived in roundhouses – circular buildings made of mud and straw, with cone-shaped roofs.

Discovery and invention

From the time people first settled in Britain, they invented things to help them survive in the harsh prehistoric landscape. As humans moved around, both within and beyond Britain, ideas and inventions spread. Over thousands of years, these were developed and improved to make life easier.

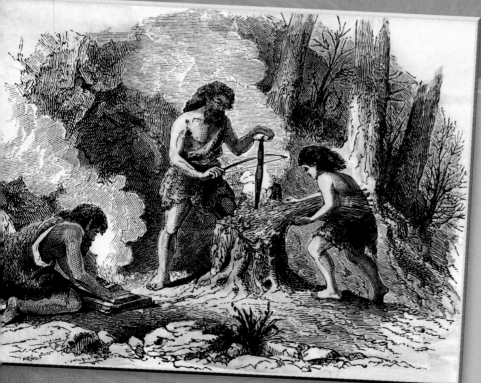

In the later Stone Age, people invented a tool called a fire drill, or bow drill, to start fires.

Controlling fire

The first people on Earth did not know how to make fire. They found branches that had been struck by lightning and used them to start a larger fire that they kept burning for as long as they could. Eventually, Neanderthals discovered that they could start a fire themselves by striking together a piece of flint and a rock that contained iron. This created sparks that could catch on dry wood or leaves to build into a blaze.

Making clothes

By discovering when head lice first evolved into clothing lice, scientists have proved that humans first wore clothes around 170,000 years ago! At this time, Europe was on the brink of an Ice Age and as the weather became colder, humans began wrapping up in animal skins. By the Bronze Age, people had learnt how to weave threads into cloth to make clothes.

By the Iron Age, clothes were similar to the way they are today. Women made the cloth using a weaving device called a loom.

Transport

The earliest wheel that archaeologists have found in Britain dates from the Bronze Age – about 3,000 years ago. The idea of the wheel had probably been around long before this. However, it was only when people worked out how to attach a platform to a set of wheels using axles that it became a really useful invention! As people learnt to tame horses, horse-drawn vehicles became an important way for traders and other travellers to get around.

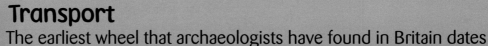

By the Iron Age, horse-drawn chariots were an important part of the battles fought between the warring Celtic tribes.

Tool technology

The two things that early humans needed to survive were food and shelter. To kill animals and build places to live, people needed tools. Simple implements made out of stone and rock have been found from as long as 700,000 years ago. They are the earliest evidence of human life in Britain.

Stone tools

Throughout the Stone Age, tools developed from simple stones sharpened on rocks, into a range of tools and weapons that could be used for different purposes. By Neolithic times, flint mining was an important industry. People dug tunnels into the earth using stone tools and picks made from deer antlers. Adults worked on the upper levels of the mines. Children were sent into the smallest, deepest tunnels to dig out the flint.

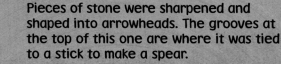

Pieces of stone were sharpened and shaped into arrowheads. The grooves at the top of this one are where it was tied to a stick to make a spear.

Early metal tools

Around 4,500 years ago, settlers from overseas introduced a new idea to Britain – a way of separating the metal copper from the rock in which it was found. Soon prehistoric people found that mixing copper with tin made a much better metal: bronze. They poured the melted metal mixture into clay moulds, then let it cool down and harden. They found that the bronze tools were much stronger than the old stone ones.

This is a clay mould for making spear tips out of bronze.

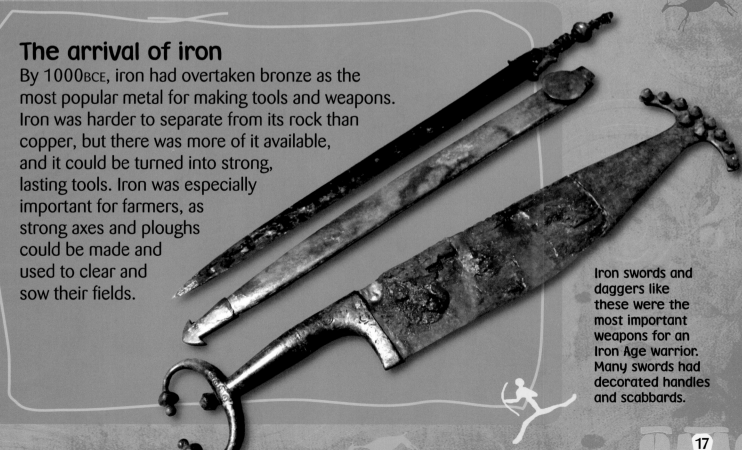

The arrival of iron

By 1000BCE, iron had overtaken bronze as the most popular metal for making tools and weapons. Iron was harder to separate from its rock than copper, but there was more of it available, and it could be turned into strong, lasting tools. Iron was especially important for farmers, as strong axes and ploughs could be made and used to clear and sow their fields.

Iron swords and daggers like these were the most important weapons for an Iron Age warrior. Many swords had decorated handles and scabbards.

Trade and travel

There was no money in prehistoric times. People did not buy things – instead they made everything they needed for their daily lives. In the days of simple stone tools and weapons, everyone made what they needed for themselves so everyone in society enjoyed equal status.

Bronze Age trade

This classless society changed when people learnt how to make things out of metal. Metalworkers were greatly respected in their social group. They had more possessions because they could trade their metal items for other things that they wanted or needed. Eventually this system of trade spread beyond local communities, and people travelled around Britain and Europe, exchanging their goods.

This is part of a Bronze Age tool called a flesh hook, which was used to remove hunks of meat from cooking pots.

Travellers from abroad

In the same way, people from other parts of the world came to Britain. The grave of a boy who was born in the Mediterranean has been found near Stonehenge. He was buried with a necklace made of amber beads that came from Scandinavia, proving that this young man had travelled a great distance before he finally reached Britain!

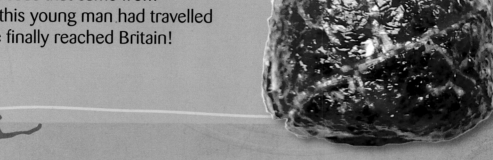

Amber beads like this were found with the body of a Bronze Age boy who was only 14 or 15 years old when he died.

The Beaker People

The Beaker People came to England from western Europe in around 2500BCE. Some historians think that it may have been the Beakers who showed people in Britain how to make bronze. Their skill with metal and pottery meant they were quickly accepted and respected by the local people. They also had their own farming methods, which people in Britain were soon using on their farms.

The Beaker People are named after the bell-shaped clay beakers they made.

Religion and ritual

Prehistoric people left no written history, so archaeologists have to examine artefacts to look for clues about what ancient people believed and how they worshipped their gods. The different ways that humans honoured the dead throughout this period also give us some ideas about their religious beliefs.

Stone Age beliefs

The fact that early people such as the Neanderthals buried their dead suggests that they had some sort of religious beliefs. Later, Mesolithic people were buried with possessions such as tools and food, so they may have believed in an afterlife where they would need these items. By the late Stone Age, many people were buried in underground tombs marked with stone monuments called dolmens or barrows.

Mesolithic headdresses like this, which looks like a pair of antlers, suggest that people carried out religious rituals.

The largest stone circle in the world, at Avebury in Wiltshire, is 420 metres across.

Stone circles

Across Britain and Europe there are many enormous stone circles that were built in Neolithic times. These may have been religious monuments, burial grounds or places believed to have special powers that could heal the sick. We know that the stone circles were important places because people travelled long distances to visit them, sometimes from abroad.

The druids

The druids (priests) were important members of a Celtic tribe. People went to them for advice on when to plant or harvest crops and many other matters. The Celts believed that druids could communicate with the gods, and they made offerings of weapons and jewellery to keep the gods happy.

Celtic druids performed religious ceremonies such as this - the ritual of oak and mistletoe.

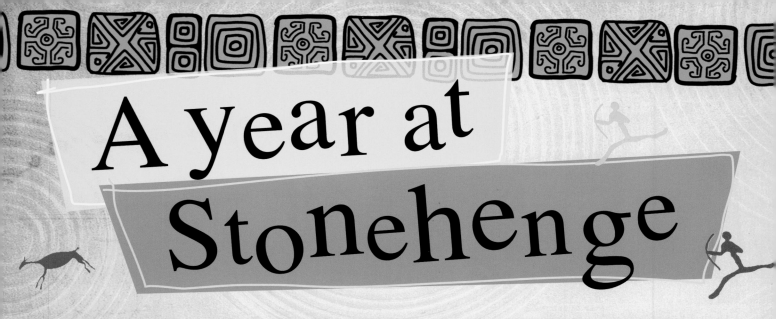

A year at Stonehenge

No one knows exactly how or why stone circles like Stonehenge were built, but one reason may have been to keep track of the seasons and mark important days in the religious calendar. This fictional diary entry describes what someone living near Stonehenge might see throughout the year.

December

The sun shining over the stone circles told us that today was the winter solstice. It is midwinter, but we celebrate the fact that spring is on its way. Hundreds of people gathered at the stones to mark the day. Later, we roasted a pig and a cow in the fire pit and had a great feast.

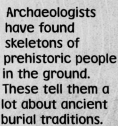

Archaeologists have found skeletons of prehistoric people in the ground. These tell them a lot about ancient burial traditions.

February

Some days ago we greeted a group of pilgrims who had come from the mountains overseas. Today one of their number, a man of about 40 years, died. We watched from a distance as he was buried in a solemn ceremony close to the great stones. A metalworker and a skilled archer, his grave was filled with arrowheads, copper knives and his anvil.

June

In the dark before dawn we moved in procession to the massive Altar Stone, and from there we watched the sun rise over the Heel Stone, heralding the summer solstice. There will be no feasting today. We know the growing season is over – the serious work of the harvest must now begin.

Arts and crafts

For thousands of years of prehistory, life was simply about survival – humans had little time for arts and crafts for their own sake. As lifestyles became more settled and tools improved, however, people began to make items that were beautiful as well as useful.

Cave paintings

Stone Age art survives in drawings and carvings on cave walls. People drew what was important to them – scenes of hunting and the animals they relied on for food. These were often made by scratching the outline and details of the animal on the rock wall using a sharp stone. The artist would then colour in the shape using charcoal or colours made from substances such as chalk (white), iron oxide (yellow) or clay ochre (red and brown).

This is one of the earliest carvings ever found. You can see the shape of a horse's head carved into a bone. It is about 12,500 years old.

24

Pottery

In the Neolithic period, people began making pottery and by the Bronze Age it had become a true craft. To begin with, people made simple bowls shaped from clay and then heated over open bonfires to dry them out. Later, kilns were built for firing the clay, and pots of all different shapes and sizes were made.

By the Bronze Age, pots were being made for all different purposes - for food and drink, for storing things, and for burying human ashes.

Jewellery

After people learnt the secrets of metalworking, they began to make decorative items. Bronze Age metalworkers beat gold into delicate thin strips that could be shaped in many ways. Later, the Celts made intricate necklaces, bracelets and brooches decorated with beautiful patterns in spirals and swirls. These items were often used to indicate someone's wealth and status.

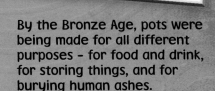

Gold was used in the Bronze Age to make jewellery and items like this cape.

25

Make a Beaker pot

People first started using clay to make pottery items in the Neolithic era. The Bronze Age Beaker people brought a different style of pottery to Britain – 'beakers' that were shaped a bit like a bell. You can make your own beaker pot using modelling clay.

You will need:
modelling clay
a rolling pin
a mug
a bowl of water
a small stick

1 Using the rolling pin, roll out some of the modelling clay to about 0.5 cm thick. Put the mug on the clay and use the stick to cut out a circle around the base.

2

Using your hands, roll the rest of the modelling clay into a long sausage about 1 cm thick. Rub some water around the edge of the clay circle, then start to coil the clay sausage around the edge of the circle.

3

Spiral upwards to build the sides of the pot until it's about 10 cm high. Build the sides outwards slightly to create the 'bowl' at the bottom, then move inwards to create the narrow 'neck' section, before moving out again at the top.

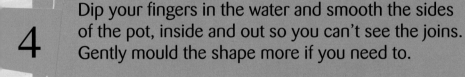

4

Dip your fingers in the water and smooth the sides of the pot, inside and out so you can't see the joins. Gently mould the shape more if you need to.

5

Using the stick, carve a series of bands around the pot about 1.5 cm apart, from top to bottom. Then use the stick to lightly carve lines, dots or patterns within each band. Finally, leave your pot to harden.

Facts and figures

There were far fewer people in Britain in prehistoric times than there are today:

Middle Stone Age: 3,000
Early Bronze Age: 20,000
Late Bronze Age: 100,000
Middle Iron Age: 250,000
Late Iron Age: 500,000
Today: 64,000,000

Avebury is the largest prehistoric site in Britain. Begun in about 2850BCE, it covers more than 11 hectares and includes three huge stone circles, one within the other.

The largest Iron Age hill fort in Britain is Maiden Castle in Dorset which was built in about 600BCE and extended 150 years later.

About 13,000 years ago, nearly three-quarters of the large animals on Earth died out. This may have been because of hunting by humans.

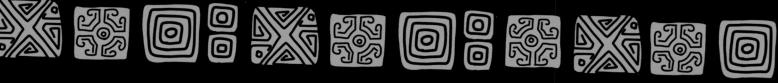

The Hallaton treasure is largest hoard of Iron Age coins discovered in Britain. It includes around 5,000 coins made of silver and gold, most of them belonging to a tribe called the Corieltauvi.

Timeline

2.5 million years ago   Start of the Stone Age

170,000BCE   People start wearing clothes

9500BCE   Last Ice Age ends

9000BCE   Start of the Mesolithic era (Middle Stone Age)

4000BCE   Start of the Neolithic era (New Stone Age)

2550BCE   The first stones are laid at Stonehenge

2500BCE   Bronze Age begins

2500BCE   Beaker people arrive in Britain

1500BCE   Causeway at Flag Fen is built

1000BCE   Wheeled transport first used in Britain

800BCE   Iron Age begins

43CE   Romans invade Britain; end of the Iron Age

29

Glossary

anvil A heavy metal block used for hammering and shaping metal.

archaeologists People who learn about the past by digging up old objects.

artefacts Objects from the past that reveal information about the people who made them.

axle A rod that runs through the centre of two wheels, joining them together.

barrow A large mound of earth or stone used as a marker for a burial site.

BCE The letters BCE stand for 'before common era'. They refer to dates before the birth of Christ.

causeway A raised road or track that runs across marshy land.

CE The letters CE stand for 'common era'. They refer to dates after the birth of Christ.

climate The weather conditions in a particular area over a long period of time.

dolmen A tomb monument made of a large flat stone on top of two upright stones.

evidence Objects, buildings or other information that show the truth about something.

flint A type of hard, grey rock used for making tools in the Stone Age.

fortified Something that has been strengthened in order to protect it from attack.

glacier A large, slow-moving river of ice.

harpoons Sharp spear-heads attached to pieces of rope, used to catch fish.

kilns Special ovens used for baking clay to harden and turn into pottery.

Mesolithic A word meaning 'Middle Stone Age' – the period from around 9000BCE to the start of the Neolithic era.

Neanderthal A species of human-like people that lived in Europe between around 120,000 years ago and 35,000 years ago.

Neolithic A word meaning 'New Stone Age' – the period from around 4000BCE to the end of the Stone Age.

Paleolithic A word meaning 'Early Stone Age' – the period from around 2.5 million years ago to about 9000BCE.

peat A sort of soil that is created when plants decay.

ritual A religious ceremony where particular actions are carried out.

scabbard A protective casing for a sword.

solstice The longest and shortest days of the year, which occur in June and December.

species A group of similar living things that are able to breed with one another.

status How important someone is, compared to other members of their society.

Further reading

Life in the Stone Age, Bronze Age and Iron Age, Anita Ganeri (Raintree, 2014)
Stone Age Bone Age! (Wonderwise), Mick Manning and Brita Granström (Franklin Watts, 2014)
Stone Age to Iron Age (The History Detective Investigates), Clare Hibbert (Wayland, 2014)
The Celts (The History Detective Investigates), Philip Steele (Wayland, 2011)

Websites

www.bbc.co.uk/history/handsonhistory/ancient-britain.shtml
A BBC website for children that describes what life was like in prehistoric times.

www.bbc.co.uk/history/interactive/games/ironage_life/index_embed.shtml
A BBC website that explains how archaeology has given us information about how people lived in the Iron Age.

www.stone-circles.org.uk/stone/
A website with a map, photographs and information about many prehistoric sites in Britain, including stone circles and hill forts.

www.theschoolrun.com/homework-help/the-bronze-age
A website containing facts, photos and links about life all over the world in the Bronze Age.

Index

Explore!

Who were the Anglo-Saxons?
Anglo-Saxon England
Anglo-Saxons and Danes
A warrior's letter
Make an Anglo-Saxon helmet
Anglo-Saxon society
Village life
Religion and belief
Technology, medicine and magic
Crafts and music
Stories, poems and riddles
The end of the Anglo-Saxons
Facts and figures
Timeline

978 0 7502 9551 2

Who were the Celts?
The Celtic world
Warrior Celts
Society and family
Everyday life
Food and farming
Technology and invention
Religion and beliefs
Festivals and fun
The tale of Cuchulainn
Arts and crafts
Make a Celtic roundhouse
Facts and figures
Timeline

978 0 7502 9550 5

What were the Stone, Bronze
    and Iron Ages?
The prehistoric world
Food and farming
Homes and buildings
Family and society
Discovery and invention
Tool technology
Trade and travel
Religion and ritual
A year at Stonehenge
Arts and crafts
Make a prehistoric cave painting
Facts and figures
Timeline

978 0 7502 9549 9

Who were the Vikings?
Viking raiders
Vikings in England
Viking society
Villages and towns
Traders and explorers
Ships and navigation
Viking beliefs
Craft, stories and music
A day in the life of a Viking child
Make a Viking loaf
The end of the Viking age
Facts and figures
Timeline

978 0 7502 9548 2

Other titles in the series

978 0 7502 8097 6

978 0 7502 8099 0

978 0 7502 8098 3

978 0 7502 8135 5

978 0 7502 8880 4

978 0 7502 8879 8

978 0 7502 8860 6

978 0 7502 8883 5